VIOLIN PLAY-ALONG

AUDIO ACCESS INCLUDED

CLASSICAL

T0084120

CONTENTS

Page	Title
2	Canon in D PACHELBEL
4	Concerto No. 1 in A Minor, First Movement J.S. BACH
8	Eine Kleine Nachtmusik ("Serenade"), First Movement MOZART
11	Flight of the Bumblebee RIMSKY-KORSAKOV
14	Hungarian Dance No. 5 BRAHMS
16	Meditation MASSENET
18	Romance in F BEETHOVEN
22	Spring, First Movement (from The Four Seasons) VIVALDI

TUNING NOTES

To access audio visit:
www.halleonard.com/mylibrary

Enter Code
2793-2656-3034-2988

ISBN: 978-1-4234-1379-0

HAL•LEONARD®
CORPORATION
7777 W. BLUEMOUND RD. P.O. BOX 13819 MILWAUKEE, WI 53213

In Australia contact:
Hal Leonard Australia Pty. Ltd.
4 Lentara Court
Cheltenham, Victoria 3192 Australia
Email: ausadmin@halleonard.com

Recorded at BeatHouse Music, Milwaukee, WI
Gerald Loughney, Solo Violin & Violin I
Cathy Bush, Violin II
Amanda Koch, Viola
Scott Cook, Cello
Wendy Prostek, Piano

Visit Hal Leonard Online at **www.halleonard.com**

Canon in D

Johann Pachelbel
for string quartet

Concerto in A Minor

I - Allegro moderato
Johann Sebastian Bach
for violin and string orchestra

Allegro moderato

cresc.

cresc.

f

dim.

p

cresc.

f

cresc.

f

dim.

p

cresc.

f

poco rit.

Eine Kleine Nachtmusik

I - Allegro
Wolfgang Amadeus Mozart
K. 525
for string quartet

Allegro

Flight of the Bumblebee

Nicolay Rimsky-Korsakov
for string quartet

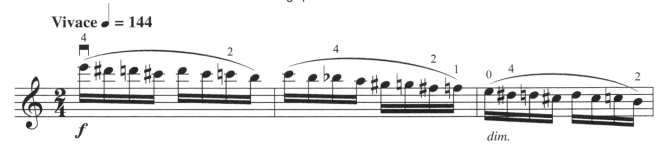

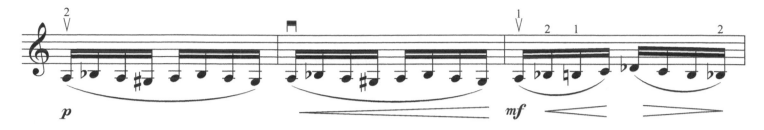

Hungarian Dance No. 5

Johannes Brahms
for violin and piano

restez (stay in
same position)

Meditation

from the opera THAÏS
Jules Massenet
for violin and orchestra

Andante religioso

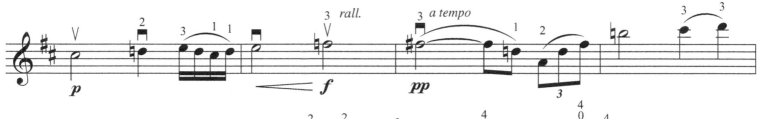

Più mosso agitato

Romance in F

Ludwig van Beethoven
Op. 50.

for violin and piano

Adagio cantabile

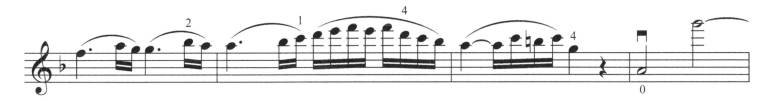

spiccato

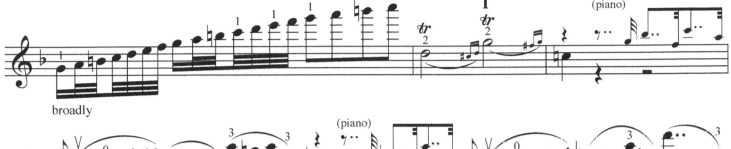

broadly

spiccato

poco rit.- - - - - - a tempo

* *(stay in same position)*

restez

(piano)

ff

play

I

*point**

dying away

* *(end of bow, opposite frog)*

Spring

I - Allegro
from THE FOUR SEASONS
Antonio Vivaldi
for string quartet

Tuoni